OCT   2015

D0871901

KIM BUI-BURTON

POETRY

COLLECTION

TRADITION

TRADITION

DANIEL KHALASTCHI

McSWEENEY'S
POETRY SERIES

811.6
KHA

McSWEENEY'S
SAN FRANCISCO

Copyright © 2015 Daniel Khalastchi

Cover art and frontispiece by Sunra Thompson

All rights reserved, including right of reproduction in whole or part in any form.

The McSweeney's Poetry Series is edited by Dominic Luxford and Jesse Nathan.

The editors wish to thank assistant editor Rachel Z. Arndt,
editorial interns Jess Bergman, Alison Castleman, Andrew Colarusso,
Caroline Crew, Lizzie Davis, Waylon Elder, Megan Freshley, Phoebe Putnam,
Neesa Sonoquie, and copyeditor Britta Ameel.

Thank you to everyone who supported the publication of this book.

McSweeney's and colophon are registered trademarks of McSweeney's,
a privately held company with wildly fluctuating resources.

Printed in the United States.

ISBN 978-1-940450-45-2

2 4 6 8 10 9 7 5 3 1

www.mcsweeneys.net

For my parents

CONTENTS

I listened. Now you listen. When the anti-Semites come to kill your mother, will it be nice to say you aren't a bar mitzvah? Don't you want to be counted?

—Leonard Michaels

PART THE FIRST

I WANT JEW SO BADLY

The conversion Rabbi comes to my door holding
a box of unwrapped dildos and a wood-handled

cement chisel. *Here*, he says, *beginning to end.* He sets
the box down on the coffee table and removes a pink

studded vibrator. Putting on cloth gloves, the Rabbi
tucks his beard into the collar of his suit shirt and

quietly tells me to get a pair of scissors. *I will only
show you this once*, he says. We spend the next hour

using Silly Putty and plastic bells to shape the
head of a traditional Jewish penis. *Circumcision,*

the Rabbi says while sweating, *will go far in creating
an identity for this child. Even if your wife never agrees*

to convert, he continues, *with the right anesthetic and a pair
of silicone earplugs, you can ignore her fevered resistance.* He smiles

and the two of us crack our knuckles. I slip up the
first few attempts at folding the foreskin, but by

the conclusion of our lesson I've gotten pretty good at
clamping, pulling, snipping, and covering the wound

with a medicated wipe. *How does it feel?* the Rabbi asks
as we break for brisket sandwiches. *Nice*, I say, *it feels*

nice to be in control of this now. I know, the Rabbi says,
handing me a towel to clear the dry pieces of rye caught

in the stubble around my mouth. *When you stop shaking,*
we can go to the basement and I'll teach you how to knock clean

Hebrew names into the dark marble of a headstone. Plus,
he says, removing a blueprint of black x's and circles

from his satin breast pocket, *if you commit to buying*
your cemetery plots today, I'll let you sleep for ten

minutes believing in the resurrection. I'd rather try
bacon, I say. *You don't want to do that,* he says.

HARD SELL OF FLAT-SCREEN
TELEVISION TO LOW-INCOME FAMILY
IN HOUSING PROJECT

For thirty-six days it rained on only
our side of the elevator. We would
leave the house. Park the car. Enter
the front doors of our common

office complex, then stop to put on
sad blue nylon raincoats. You would
hold the umbrella more over your
body but there was really no

escape. A series of thunders
choked through the hallway each
time we made the service call. The
fluorescent lights strung overhead

sweated and dripped in the sudden
humidity. Some of those afternoons
I'd find you naked in the break room
asking an undocumented Korean janitor

if this horrible pattern was because of
the abortion. Your neck bones laddered
in the shape of Anne Frank. On the
thirty-seventh day, we began to take

the stairs. On the thirty-eighth, you
strangled a horse and hid for a year
not breathing in its muscle.

POSTERIOR CRUCIATE SONNET

You empty the contents of the vacuum

    cleaner bag into two separate

smaller bags that we put around our mouths and

    huff until one of us passes out. I never see you

fall from your crutches, but that's because very

    quickly I'm on the tile floor, drool

and teeth spilling over the small carpet squares we keep

    piled in front of the refrigerator. When I

stand up, you ask me to participate in various

    competitions of skill and agility to prove considerable

brain function and also that I'm

    not a pussy. For an hour, I carry duffel

bags full of your sanitary waste to the river with

    flashlights stapled to my shoulders and a

bullhorn rallying my breath. Afterward, I sleep

       with the neighbor while you show her kid a

hot functioning menorah. When the cops

       come, I give everybody gifts I purchased in

the beauty of unheralded economic

       decline. Your present is by far the

most anticipated. You don't open it right

       away, but it's clear by morning you've figured

out how to put it all together. If the jetpack works, get

       quick to a city and buy into a co-op. I will

only come looking for you once I've found a way to

       steal a mobile home and family. Look at me

in these white gloves. I am a terrible thief

       and yet.

ON THE QUESTION OF OUR WEIGHT

We fucked two days ago
our last exit opportunity: large
cave, small light, loud

voices, a rockslide. Once
the dust settled, there was
quite a bit of time for honest

conversation. I started
by telling you about
a suburban wig factory for

house pets, and you
responded by saying your
mother was no longer

menstruating. I tried to
switch the topic to proper
parking lot etiquette but you

interrupted, methodically listing
four specific examples in which
you believed female castration

was an appropriate form of
cultural obstinance. When I
agreed, you stopped

breathing. Your right jab came
quickly, but to be fair, in that thick
darkness I never had the chance

to react. An hour passed before
you asked if I was bleeding, and
when I couldn't answer

you struck me again. *Do you
think,* you said later, our air
depleting while we shared

the last throat lozenge, *that male
high school girls' basketball
coaches feel their athletes are*

*the reason they have such distance
in their marriages? I don't
know*, I said. *I do*, you

said, and you began to
dig us a tunnel with your
teeth—such beauty

in the coughs and gags I
never heard the walls give
in to our grief.

FEMININE HUSTLE

We are in a bus. We are under
a plane. We are in a bus
under a plane, and that plane
is on fire. Everyone is

silent. We are
screaming. We are
screaming at everyone
for being silent. Everyone

is screaming. The windows
in the bus are not
breaking. The bus has
no windows not breaking but

we are in it still together
with bags of stolen vitamins and
receipts for powerful glasses. We have
enough glasses for the handicapped

passengers but when you stand up
to deliver our announcement the
bus driver sees that you are
bleeding. We are all

bleeding. We are all blood and
moisture and the bus is
full of it but none of us are
wet. You and I are told to

put on sad blue nylon
raincoats. The people
in the bus are in
that bus. They are under

a plane, a plane on fire, and we
are on the side of the road
in a ditch with a pair of
hands-free flashlights shining

like a kettle of breath. There are
people in a bus and people
in a plane. We are not in
either of them. We are looking

for dinner. We are catching
raccoons. We are saving the
meat in your pocketed scarf and
there is a bus. There is a plane. There

is electricity in a house on a hill
handsome in the distance.

TECHNICALLY, I CAN APPLY FOR FOOD STAMPS

You set out a shoebox and bait
the cardboard walls with a ring

of dried angleworms and thinly sliced
ground beetles. I watch you climb a

dying birch tree and when you come
down you tell me, *don't*

worry, don't worry, I swear I know
what I'm doing. And what

would that be? I ask. *Catching*
robins, you say, pulling my

bad arm as we run inside the
house, binoculars and a pack of

benzocaine condoms hanging
from your neck. Throughout

the day we fuck and sing and
watch from a window to see

if your trap yields any
worthwhile results. In late

afternoon, after the engine
of locusts has gone suddenly

quiet, I ask how you figure
this plan pans out. *There's no*

lid, I say. *No string. The birds*
can eat and eat and

eat through the night and
when we wake up, sweaty

and bored, having lost
more hair and hours of

breathing, the birds will be
full, strung high on a

wire. Your smile is
weak as you pat at my

back. *There, there,* you
say. *I poisoned the*

worms with varying levels of
carbofuran. It took me

weeks to weigh the dosage but
if my math is correct, every fifteen

steps there should be more
death. I rest my

face in your chest. *Why are we*
doing this? I ask. *You are so*

hungry, you say. *Won't*
the chemical affect us? I ask. *It*

doesn't matter, you say. *Wear*
these gloves. Take this

bag. Don't ever say we aren't trying.

HOW I HAVE LEARNED TO DEAL
WITH MY VANITY

You knit me a consolation scarf and leave it
on my side of the slowly deflating air mattress
after one of our less insightful meetings with the

therapist. The scarf is black and troubling, and
as I try it on for your bad eyes behind the
camera, you admit the bulk of its sad thickness

is constructed from my thinning hair. Tying it
around my neck, I smell the dry cucumber and
mentholated soothing agent of my rinse-away

conditioner. Once I am reacquainted with its
weight, I move into the bathroom and make
the mirror make me take a shot at changing

style. Over the next few hours, you explain
the scarf is fragile—that the more I pull and
loosen, the more I'll recognize the fallout. I

tell you I don't think you've thought completely
through the metaphor, but I also ask you not to
adjust your position in the doorway. *You're*

blocking the right amount of light, I say. *That's*
flattering, you say. *You know what I mean,* I
say. *Do I?* you say. *Come on,* I say. *I'm almost*

thirty—I can't hold a steady job and the failure's
made me rich with dermatitis. There have been days
when you aren't here that I reuse your Q-tips. I am

afraid, I continue, *that this is full catastrophe*
living. You take the scarf and wrap its dark trail
around your sunk and weathered frame. *Is this*

how we look at parties, I say, pointing back at our
reflection, *the crowded space between us always headed*
toward disaster? You don't answer. The next

morning, we are shadowed with bruises and the
possibility of having lost another baby. You have
never felt, we agree, ever more alive.

MISSPENT GENDER SONNET

It sounded like a parade—like twenty-seven

    badly played instruments and a middle-aged

white woman waving from the back of a

    refurbished convertible—but it

wasn't a parade. It was constructed

    malfeasance: a missing guardrail, a risen

lake, a felled night left hacking its way

    through the city, a relay team of high

school boy cheerleaders driving to a bridal shop in

    an attempt to see what happens when

a person gives up. You heard it first but

    by the time I registered the music as

the siren that it was, you had already assured me how

    lucky we were to live with such a large

amount of culture. After you climbed back into

bed, we talked about your shoulder, how

you dislocated it often during sex because

you liked the sharp pain and what it did

for your memory. We fell asleep to televised surgery

but sometime near dawn I woke to hear

you singing a song about ambulances and cliffs and

a man pushing a grocery cart full of tin

cans past an empty stretcher waiting for a

helicopter to drop another wet body

recovered by the divers. Your tone was soft

and you were patient like a newscaster. *There*

are no doctors, you sang in your teddy. *There are no*

doctors, and this wasn't an accident.

NOTES FROM AN ADJUNCT PROFESSOR AT A MAJOR AMERICAN UNIVERSITY

You make a cross of split
forks and cedar and hang it
on the wall to protect me
while I teach. When I ask

what you are afraid of, you
remove a list from the inside
pocket of your purse and begin
to read with great thunder

and silence—*pregnancy*
pacts, you say; *boys with white*
hands following you home; ball-
gags; panic in a crowd; wet

spoons; that they'll find out you're
Jewish; the Internet; glycerin
soap; rap music; an increasing over-
sexualization of aging men in positions

of influence; what they will offer
in your office; what you will offer
in your office; their legs; your
immaturity; a natural disaster in

which you give your lunch to a group
of college freshman so they can survive
an extra forty-eight hours and you die
a slow, emaciating death; a car

wreck; leaving town; how many of
them admit to anal sex; de-
humidifiers; group addiction
therapy; insurance conventions; and

pregnancy pacts. I never ask
about the repetition, but you
confess later, at an Italian
restaurant, that the most

frightening thing, the most
terrifying thing, the thing
that keeps you from leaving
the house when I invite you

to magic shows, is that some-
where along the line you've
agreed to carry an unspecified
man's baby. You say you know

the call is coming. That you
can't back out. That you
are sure when I see you
sick in the mornings I will

take the dog, the long gray
Chrysler, and leave after
speaking very authoritatively
on the nature of fidelity. *But*

how would I know it isn't mine? I
ask, rubbing my palms against
the raise of my wallet. *That's
why I made you this*

cross, you say. *Sometimes, I pray
my uterus just collapses.*

WHAT WE ARE NOT

I never paid for anything. Even the dinners we split down the middle, and when your nursing-home grandmother called I was quiet like you asked. In fact, most of the time we just talked about leaving. How the city was filling you sick like a gutter, and why you thought brown bears would be scarier with longer tails. Usually, before we touched, you put on lip-gloss and shook loose your sandals to the floor of my Nissan. In the dashboard light, your eyes seemed to break wide cycles of shadow. They stayed open when I whistled your shoulder. Open when I lifted your shirt with my teeth. Open when I laid you across the center console, your knees pressed together like refusing a birth. We always stayed in the driveway because you never wanted to come inside. *My pretty bag*, I'd call you, *my beautiful case of land-worked suffrage*. When you and your post-rehab boyfriend finally have your agnostic-based commitment ceremony, I will go to an unclaimed beach house and pretend to read *Nazi Literature in the Americas* in front of a Yeshiva boys' primary school science class. I imagine them in a circle with yarmulkes and smut magazines, calculating a range of possible intrauterine temperature shifts by filtering sand through cracked beakers and paper. Most of the kids will seem happy by that water.

JEW AND I TRAVEL TO THE BEAT OF
A DIFFERENT DRUM

The conversion Rabbi takes me to a remodeled Clinique
counter and tells me to enjoy the samples. I use the scruffing

lotion, the intense hydrating moisturizer, and after a few
minutes of informative blackhead discussion with two elderly

female aestheticians, we tweeze my eyebrows and thank
everyone for their time. *You look rested,* the Rabbi says as we

situate our gift bags in the trunk of his Lincoln. *You look fierce
and assertive and that's going to help when we get to shul.* For the rest

of the afternoon I am treated to hand-jobs and head
massages. We go to a Russian bath, a suit-fitting, and end

the day stripped of our shirts, discussing flattering wet/dry
hairstyles with a barberette we call "Tina." I ask for a hot

shave but the Rabbi shakes his head. *We need to show you have
the soul of a carburetor. Shaving,* he continues, *is the mark of a man*

who still has a mother. The Rabbi tells Tina to put the day's
services on his tab, and we take a rough road back to the

synagogue and park. While I futz with the radio, the Rabbi
reaches into his breast pocket and removes a thick manila

envelope beating with cash. *Get out,* he says, and we walk to
the rear exit of the building and position my body to look

naturally negligent. It is hard to stand with my feet facing
each other, but I am assured with confidence this is how

things must begin. Before he leaves, the Rabbi stuffs my
pants and mouth with crisp new money and a Sinatra

cassette. *When the ladies come out of Maariv, they will fight to see who
gets to take you home. But I already have a wife,* I mumble through

the paper. *These women won't care,* the Rabbi says. *They will make
you apricot kugel and strong babies and the whole time they'll only be*

thinking how much they are lifting themselves to the Lord.

THE ADMITTANCE OF PERSONAL
INVESTMENT

We send letters that begin with little-known facts about the Holocaust. *Dear you,* you say, *even though the mass extinction of your people never happened, it would have nonetheless been justified because the Jews are an alien, parasitical race, hell-bent on destroying the noble Aryan and/or defiling his blood, etc. I miss you and hope to be out of the hospital soon.*

~

Dear you, I respond, *the Jewish people were a scapegoat for the collapse of Germany after WWI. Also,* I add, *the word "Holocaust" is derived from the Greek words "completely" and "burnt." If there were no Holocaust, how do you explain why so many Jews still will not buy Volkswagens? I am sorry to hear you are in the hospital. Please take care to bring yourself health.*

~

Dear you, you say, *in the winter of 1936 your people, the Jews, were practicing incest. They lived together in tight quarters and the German government was concerned about disease. These people were brought to open spaces where they could work, and sleep, and have consistent access to showers. There never were gas chambers, but even if there were, they only existed to fumigate clothing or to help calmly end the lives of those suffering from* typhus. Thank you for your well wishes—the growths have been removed. We are all now hoping that the vomiting will cease.

~

Dear you, I respond, *it is estimated that one point five million children died during the Holocaust. Of that one point five million, roughly one point two million were Jewish, the rest Gypsy children who were forced to sleep with animals. These children were separated according to their age: children infant to age six were grouped together, as were children seven to twelve, and teenagers thirteen to seventeen. Jewish students were affected by the "Law Against Overcrowding in German Schools and Universities." Jewish children could never surpass one point five percent of the total students in a given school. The Nazis were flushing out the young so they could not grow to overpower them. We never had children but surely you remember watching the neighborhood boy die of leukemia. It is rotten to eat the food of an inner-city hospital. Notify the doctors that upon your release, I will do what I can to care for you.*

~

Dear you, you say, *if no written order for the Holocaust can be found, then Hitler never gave the order. Furthermore, Jewish women and children were partisans, or were guilty of committing heinous crimes, or both. There is even strong evidence to suggest these mothers were looking for a way to escape their marriages, and any argument against this theory displays an irrational reluctance to accept the basic principles of precautionary grief. These things, I'm afraid, you will never allow yourself to see. My eyes are not what they used to be. When I look at pictures of our time inside the courthouse, I have to ask the orderlies why you are made of vinyl siding.*

~

Dear you, I respond, if the majority of recorded speeches from this time period were faked, and if all other similar documentation (such as photographs and films) were also faked, and if Himmler's 1943 Posen speech (which was recorded and transcribed) wasn't really his voice, or parts were added later, or the technology to record didn't exist in 1943, or it disagrees with Himmler's notes for the speech, then I can understand the impulse to entertain the idea of a cover-up. But to think the victims were responsible for what happened is putting too much stock in a people who always believed that divine intervention would keep them from such gloaming affliction. When I talk to my parents, they are clear about their desire for me to marry a believer of the faith—I'll settle for someone who believes faith is possible. There is to be some weather during my flight back to the city. Our land has been secured. We will be a wonderful family in light of this news.

PART THE SECOND

HORMONE ELEVATION SONNET

You wake me up saying, *hurry, hurry, grab the*

chainsaw. I don't think we

have a chainsaw, but you point

to the corner where I usually keep

my salon-quality hair loss treatment and I

follow you, back-bent through the stair-

well, revving steel teeth against a full-set night. When

we get to a gas station, you ask

for some money and tell me that

whenever the moon is so

low and in focus you feel like a Chinese

war prisoner pulling live

mice through a collapsing

urinal hole. In my pockets, I don't

have any money. I try to

      apologize but you just sit on the

curb listing all the better sexual

      experiences you've had until I realize, finally,

what the chainsaw

      is for. A few minutes

later, I bring you a bag of cash, three wet

      cartons of cigarettes, and a thick black

T-shirt with a fanged howling wolf

      ironed on in profile. *With all the*

commotion, I say, *I never got to check the size. It's*

      okay, you respond. *Sometimes my*

breasts remind you of terriers. These

      are the things we can sell to the sheriff.

POLICE REPORT ECLOGUE

The night-shift clerk says that when he came to, we'd already dismantled the security tapes and urinated in the silver troughs kept out for the continental breakfast. When I came to, I was tied to a guardrail on a highway near the river. The lump on my head was smaller than his, but the police have confirmed the trauma was caused by the same blunt instrument—a collapsible colander or a cast-iron milk pan. After their insinuation, I rose to your defense. I told them about your shoulder, how when driving at night you felt like a long loaded handgun with terrible depth perception, and how I was certain that whoever put you up to this had threatened my safety, or had brought up your father, and that you would come back for me soon wearing a dark suede cowboy vest with a plea bargain sewn to its lapel. Before I got to the part about how I also believed the handcuffs themselves were a strong indication that you had been compromised, taken hostage by a rogue rookie cop trying to make a name for himself, they handed me your letter. I didn't open it right away, but when I did I was struck by the weak calligraphy. *It is my fault,* you began, *that when we read celebrity news magazines I make you whistle the theme song from the rolling credits of* Schindler's List. *I know that film is difficult because of the unnecessary color shifts and determined overacting, but the thought of it now supports an underlying suspicion that my habit for purchasing bruised organic produce at the gluten-free cooperative is an aversion defense response to a feared social interaction I am certain still awaits me at the more economical supermarket. Please tell the man from the motel this was not about our service. I will send for you soon. Do not let him sleep by the light of that window.*

PRAYING WHILE THE PLANE GOES DOWN

You want to eat dinner naked
while watching my bar mitzvah
video. I tell you we can watch
the video, but being naked this

close to where they botched
my circumcision makes me un-
comfortable. You laugh and ask
where we are. I point to a

map, then to a house on the
map, then to a picture of my
grandparents in denim-lined
coffins. The picture is over-

exposed, but you compliment
its composition and suggest that
because of the dirt piled loose
along his forehead, my grand-

father looks like an older version
of an institutionally young
Hispanic politician. I tell you
to eat your soup. You look

confused and I apologize numerous
times before locking myself in the
bathroom where for roughly an
hour I practice wearing oversized

jewelry and setting my hair with
ceramic hot curlers. I'm embarrassed
by my behavior, and I tell you so
in a note I slide under the door to

where you wait with Xanax and
a carnival of jagged ships you've
fashioned from the less-expensive
china. *I am embarrassed*, I write. *I*

know, you respond. *No*, I write, *I*
am embarrassed and nonassertive and
my ankles look like frozen bags of
teeth inside these tapered jeans. But

we've been over this, you say, and as
a gesture of concession I remove
my swollen tonsils with a matchbook
and your tweezers. After we

determine what is really worth the
screaming, I tape the raw red
tissue in a hole behind the
shower where I find an unsealed

envelope containing two worn
keys and a scrambled
address for a mannequin ware-
house built adjacent to the

synagogue. *I am afraid*, you say
later, *that I've misinterpreted what it is
we are doing in this house.* I want to
tell you that you haven't but

then everything is dark.

I WOULD JEW ANYTHING FOR LOVE

With very rigid movement, the conversion Rabbi takes me
into a restaurant bathroom to rob men of their wallets while

they attempt to use the urinal. At first I protest, but once the
Rabbi explains the events as a character-building exercise, I

go all-in with the gusto of a B-list method actor on the set
of a sound-staged Western. *Give up the goods,* I say. *Nice,* the

Rabbi whispers. *Fuck you, pay me,* I growl. *Again, strong presence,*
the Rabbi says, *but there's no need to be vulgar. We've got your*

daughter tied up with her pants … I begin, but before I can finish
the Rabbi slaps my throat and apologizes to the victim for my

utter indecency. It isn't until we start our long drive back
to the suburbs that I ask about the video surveillance and

corroborating stories likely to find their way to the cops. *We*
weren't wearing masks, I say, sweat rolling down my torso and

legs, *they could make your beard from a helicopter. This is true,* the
Rabbi responds, *but you are forgetting what we have a right to*

after the Holocaust. I'm not sure what you mean, I say, but the Rabbi
quiets my lips and laughs at a tollbooth worker as we pass

without paying. *I feel for the first time,* he says, *like you are under-*
standing how to pitch this religion. Rabbi, I say, *I think I've been shot.*

ALL THE UNEMPLOYED ARTISTS
I KNOW HAVE iPHONES

We walked to the sea with a bucket

and a hand rake. We dug out our

kidneys, put them in the bucket, then

waited for rain you said the weather-

man promised. On the beach, we lay

tangled like the leashes of euthanized

house pets, red trails from our bodies

tied together at points, then keeping

a passionate, rational distance. You

passed out first but before you did

your moan—your wheeze, your

attempts to prove that we'd been

foolish in thinking this kind of illiterate

protest would garner any significant

attention from my already uninterested

family—was lost in the knuckle and waste

of some cars along the highway. Still, your

gasps were perfectly pitched—a string of

low sharps and minors that left me quietly

thinking about the theme song from

Mr. Belvedere. Where we dropped the rake

your sunhat sat resting next to a hole-cut

sheet I couldn't quite reach. As you began

your seizure, I thought: *we just might live*

the good life yet.

DEAR PAST

We were aiming for a deer but instead hit a highway patrolman and the little boy he had pinned down in the brush with his shoulder. From where we were kneeling, we could see only the blood and the legs and the superhero underwear hanging from a branch some thirty yards away. You wanted to poke them with our rifle, but I suggested using the Q-tips we brought with us to keep the barrel clean. Together we leaned close and busied ourselves in the smell of wet leather and Kevlar. We stayed there until the sky ran white, watching a raccoon take unsalted peanuts you'd placed in the mouth of the officer's right hand. When I stopped vomiting, you told me that regardless of the evidence, the state would never convict on a charge where its own negligence factored into the depreciation of natural survival skills. We were thirteen. Our bar mitzvah was terrible. You made me try to lick the mole on the backside of our scrotum during the wedding anniversary of a cousin in Skokie, and we stole a camera.

EMERGENT OCCASION SONNET

You put a red-winged black-

      bird inside the exhaust

manifold of my 1985 Buick

      Skylark, and when I start

the engine the bird has

      babies. We receive similar

results using a three-legged

      rabbit, but when you place

large amounts of cash against the hollow

      metal carriage, our arms are

suddenly broken and you encourage

      further experimentation. Using

my mouth to roll the ignition, for the next

      fifteen minutes we experience

transitive decay. Teeth are

        lost. You swallow

your tongue. I see my knee-

        caps stack along the gear shift, but at

your insistence I keep turning the

        key. Later that afternoon, when

we are just salivating box fans

        offending the neighbors, you

ask what it feels like to irrigate a

        village using plastic animal

ribs. *The only time I've*

        done it, I say, *it felt like a theater. A*

theater? you say. *Like a theater, with*

        a tunnel, leading to a crime.

THE SUCCESS OF THOSE AROUND ME

After a city bus struck our local North
American Auto Workers for Lower Flood
Insurance Premiums Children's Choir, we

decided to hold a rally. It wasn't difficult
to reserve the fairgrounds, but finding
a group of homely young professionals

to stage an interpretive reenactment
of the accident proved harder than
anyone expected. In the end, you

suggested we hire the Tri-City Adopted
Jewish Women's Vocal Quartet, who agreed
in principle to lip-synch a recording we

had of our former lead soloist singing
"My Baby Just Cares for Me" in a factory
bathroom during last year's safety awards

ceremony. Hearing that voice again from
the grandstand speakers was incredibly
persuasive. Before we left for the after-

party, a pregnant woman asked you to sign
her stomach with a thermometer. You never
wanted children. But in that moment.

LOVER, JEW SHOULD HAVE COME OVER

Exiting the maxivan, I see the conversion Rabbi standing
before a large suburban Costco with two Ziploc baggies and

a bottle of antacids. *Here*, he says, *today we join the struggle.* I
take a deep breath and busy myself in the fields of my coat

pockets as the Rabbi shows the doorman his membership
card. Once inside, we make our way to the restroom, putting

on gray wigs and oversized reading glasses in front of an
aluminum mirror with only vague reflective properties. From

what I can tell, we look like widowed physical education
teachers at a graduation party, but the Rabbi assures me our

disguises are more than suitable for the day's activity. I try to
ask a few questions, but the Rabbi covers my ears and kicks

open the door with the heel of his Rockports. Across all
aisles, senior citizens pushing walkers and Chanel-covered

oxygen bags are roaming for food samples. Like the Rabbi
they hold plastic sacks and stomach relaxers and it becomes

clear as we make our way through the building that many are
saving the non-perishable items in case their grandchildren

decide to visit. I feel sick from the smell of Polident and
chicken liver, but the Rabbi gives me a mint and tells me to

stop staring at the floor. *If your wife won't cook for you*, he says as
we enter the frozen meat section, *you'll have to learn to feed in the*

wild. There is a brief paramedic disruption, but eventually we
begin our crusade; we line up, and start by eating an entire

Hebrew National salami with toothpicks and hand-scored
Triscuits. We taste the corned beef, the mixed veal and turkey

Vienna hot dogs, and at one point I think I see the Rabbi
push a handful of iced V8 juice into the zippered section of

his wallet. By late afternoon, the Rabbi feels I've learned my
lesson and pulls me aside to study a cookbook endorsed by a

celebrity talk show host. *Look*, he says with his hand on my
thigh, *if you ask one of the workers for salt, we'll have everything we*

*need to make this Grits and Cow Tongue Salsa. But I don't like
grits*, I say, picking fresh lettuce from the root of my bi-

cuspid. *Yes you do,* the Rabbi responds. *Sometimes these things
aren't all about race.*

LOVE, AND HONOR, AND PITY, AND PRIDE, AND SELF-DEPRECATING VERBAL SPARRING

Checking to see if our neighbors care for your safety,

we open the windows. Every few minutes, we put

our faces close to the breathable screens and yell out

what we think will gain attention: *I have a knife! You*

are a racist! I sleep with your uncles because you don't

satisfy me! Et cetera. It's your idea to soak a piece of

plywood in the bathtub overnight and hit it with the

palms of our hands so it sounds like someone is being

slapped in the neck. Each time we do it I can tell it

turns you on and at one point—after you scream, *you*

son of a bitch, I hope you kill me so they put you in jail after a

long drawn-out celebrity trial and you spend the rest of your

life giving cups of clean urine to a cellmate who has a fetish for

horses and makes you whinny while he rubs your back—I think you might even ask me to hold you. But you

don't. Instead, we spend what's left of the afternoon

breaking dishes and tearing up photocopies of our

marriage contract, and when the cops don't come and

we're pretty sure everyone is asleep, we turn on the Golf

Channel and shut all the windows. Cleaning up the next

morning, I find a piece of your dried cuticle and a note

on the table asking me to make sure I have no visible

bruises. In a bag by the door is a rope and two Ziploc

freezer bags. When I see them, I run around the house

screaming, *North Dakota, North Dakota, North Dakota.*

COARSE DERIVATIVE ACTION

In defense of further mistreatment, we break apart

the barn doors and remove from your red backpack

a depth-adjusting nail gun fully swaddled in used

newsprint. Though the heat and dried animal feces

smell more pleasant than expected, I am reluctant to

admit it when you force me to my knees. Wearing cheap

commissioned jean shorts, you stand over me for hours

feeding nothing but the night—our shadows, a tall stalk

leaning toward a chicken, the angle of light making

small-necked pastors of the nails you keep in a bucket

on your hip. A few minutes before you shoot me in the

shoulder, you hand me a list of things to say that I don't

wholeheartedly agree with: *I have no power*, I mutter. *My skin*

is not repulsive. Religion is only a way for parents to rationalize their

behavior with other local couples on a booze cruise in the Caribbean after their children hear about it from a school guidance counselor. What

else? you say. *Nothing,* I say, *that's all you've written down. Are you*

sure? you say. *It doesn't suggest anything about my bone*

structure? About how I remind you of sad horses in a field

running under a crop duster, twitching and blinking while they

choke on pesticides? I'm pretty sure this is a trick and I take

a long time deciding how to answer. When I finally

look up, you pull against the trigger. *You are a strong*

woman, I say calmly. *You and those horses feel nice in the dark.*

OSCILLATING DISTURBANCE SONNET

When it's dark, you lie under the carcass

    of a half-deer we find in a ditch along the

highway and wait for my parents' maroon

    minivan to get close. Every few

minutes I hear you vomit from the smell of bug-

    ridden intestines, but this was your

idea and I've learned not to stand in the way during

    such extreme examples of a point

not being made. Twice I crawl up next

    to you and ask if we can change

the subject, and each time you respond with

    sighs, repeating a line about having

read enough psychical research to understand

    the basic human response to young

agnostic women claiming they

are apparitions. *But you're not*

a ghost, I say, and then we see the head-

lights. Judging by the hicks and flats

of your back, you appear to be laughing as you walk

to the center of the road. It's difficult

to hear everything you're saying, but when

you stop to face the traffic, I see you are

clenching the deer's front right hoof in your teeth. *This*

is disgusting, I say. *Mmhmm*, you

say. *We're out of water*, I say, but you don't

respond, the animal tongue resting

on your forehead like

an avenue of tables.

PART THE THIRD

POEM FOR MY FATHER

I.

It was the year after
        your family

    moved to the
        city. At the Frank

Iny school for
        Jewish children in

        Baghdad, you sung
    what you heard

        on American
            radio while

        classmates danced low in
            the heat of

    wool socks. There
        was a girl you

knew but I don't
            know what you

        did with her. I
            do know that

when her brother came
    home with letters he

    said you'd written his
    sister, you didn't

deny it. He called you
    kike or *ka-*

fir dhimmi or what-
    ever Muslim boys said to

Jews like you in Iraq
    in the 1960s. When Uncle

    Salman found out, he
    un-set your jaw with his

belt buckle. Your father was
    dead. You left that

    night and on the banks
    of the Tigris you caught a small

scattering bird with your feet.

II.

You walked until morning. The city was
swollen in throngs of long cotton and the

souqs became veined with lines for raw
meat. Standing in garbage, you needed

new clothes. Back at your house, a police-
man was waiting with sandals by the

door. He asked for ID and if you were
Jewish. From your wallet fell pictures

of a well-dressed man. Before taking you
away, the officer spoke to an onlooking

neighbor. What she said in her garden let
him let you go.

III.

You   thought you were   being
    followed so   again you   walked

    the city. You   moved through
crowds with   your hands in

    your pockets. From   radios and
        bullhorns came   talk of

nation-traitors. In   Liberation   Square
    eleven   or   nine or

    eight bruised Jews hung   from crude
        gallows   all   rotted and

            stiff.   The
        accounts   differ.   I

    haven't been   able to
            ask you about it.

IV.

Based on the   discolored flesh, it
    is thought that   some of the
victims were tortured   in prison long
    before their verdicts   came down. When
you saw the   hanging bodies you
    didn't then know   that you had
shared dinner with   one at a
    wedding. You did   know a friend's
father had been   captured and re-
    leased. That night   he was found
        spread wide on   a sidewalk, holding
            pulled rice with   a nail in his head.

V.

I am saying you left
soon after because

you won't tell me what
happened. I know Uncle

Haron let you
sleep in his

kitchen. I know he
arranged for your

passage through
mountains, and

I know you
dreamt in hot

sweats for a
week. I imagine you

lying in the bed of a
truck holding wooden

toy rifles with a
blanket pulled over

your face. At checkpoints
I think of you slowing

your breath. Later, I'm
told, you rode a blind donkey

while a man who was
with you kept violently

coughing. Somehow,
from the border, you sent

word in a letter.

VI.

Snow. Mud.   Leaves. Either
way, your   letter to   Mamma
Jackie was   full of
covered ground.   You
had traveled two   hundred and
seventy miles.   The   tracks be-
hind you sunk   deep in a
storm and   wind rocked   pieces of
night   at your   neck.   In
careful Arabic you   wrote *hard*
water the   earth sings   my
ankles awake. Reading it   now there
is loss of   translation. You seem
to be   asking for   cloth or
a jacket. You
were in a new   country where
there was new   language and
you signed   your name by
swearing your mother.

VII.

From what I can piece
together, here's what

happens next: you
surrender to Iranian

authorities, are locked
in a room so you can be

questioned, then brought
to Tehran where you

board your first
plane. You land in

Tel Aviv to hands with
no rings. They put you

in *ulpan*. Give you
to the army. You fight

in a war, meet an
American, ask her to

watch your records
and dishes, promise

to return when you are
on leave. Then

you _____.

VIII.

Only after _____ do you
decide to get married. Because

the ceremony will be held in the
States, her family flies to Israel

where you are first introduced
to the people you unhappily work

with for the next some thirty-odd
years. Soon, your wife moves you

to Middle America and you save
what you can for a Renault and a

carport. Surrounded by boxes of
pre-engineered sheet metal, you wait

to start building.

IX.

The rest of your   life played out
like you   feared: your   mother

died. You stopped   talking to
family. You   did not

visit   Israel for ten
full years and   you kept

buying   cigarettes. You
grew a thick   mustache. Began

playing golf. Saw   doctors and
doctors and   nothing would

help so   you made two children
and hated your job. You   watched

television. Never   spoke
Arabic. You bought a small

car, put   down your   dog, drove
one friend to prison, and had

a large fire. Your children
left. Your stomach   got

hot. You went   to more
doctors and   your wife

stopped   driving. You
got sick. Got   better. Got

sick. Got   better. Got
sick. Got sick.   Got

rid of your colon.   Now your
days are unpatiently gray. Your

ostomy bag leaks.   Your son stayed
gone. Your daughter

had a   daughter you
hold and you   cover and

sometimes   you whisper
without even   breathing *she-*

hecheyanu v'   *kiyimanu*   *v'*
higi'anu laz'man   *hazeh* and I'm

not   entirely sure you
ever really   mean it.

FUNEREAL DISEASE

Thirty-two. That's how many
keys I can fit in my mouth
and still drink a glass of water
without choking. I've done it

twice. Once for a group of
friends who had all gone through
long-punishing divorces. The second
time, I was alone. The lights were

off and the cars from the city
seemed heavy away. All our keys
were piled on the kitchen table: the
consumption key, the dare-not key, the

key to your Spanish muralist's beach
house, the key to the drawer where
we stored more keys. I could have
kept going but the shaped metal against

my exposed fillings made me shudder and
retch. For six years, I've been wearing
this ski mask and counting to one hundred
in short, even breaths as a way of keeping

us together. I am told in this outfit
I walk like a man in pageant shoes. I feel
like a champion not running to look.

FISCAL AMBULATORY RESPONSE

When you are old. When you are older. When you are too old to be perceived as even partially attractive—your skin a concentrated map of spotted concentration camps, your hair replaced by weathered birds sedated in a storm—I will live still in the panic of the house we shared collapsing. Because of this untethered fear, I often fall asleep behind your headboard with a hatchet and wake to find you bleeding from your torso on the floor. According to my recent conversations with the doctor, you will die sometime before me not because of all the cancer, but because you have a blind mistrust for faith in times of crisis. There is something quite appealing about walking from commitment when tradition says the horse inside our bathtub isn't there. In a letter from Vancouver, you ask with your new accent how we could ever raise a family. In response, I tell you only what I know to be the truth: when you are old. When you are older. When you are too old to believe that we should never have been neighbors, I will build for us a library of celebrated failures and fill it with work that assures you.

RAVENOUS REGULATORY
TRANSITION SONNET

We ride horses along the highway, stopping

      whenever possible to replace each wooden

telephone and electrical pole we see with strikingly

           similar composite poles that are roughly

twenty feet shorter in length. As I chop

      away at their bases, using my shoulder

and forefoot to brace against the drawing

           weight, you tell me stories of bestiality

and activist espionage, pausing at turns

      to remark that with my utility lineman's

gloves and welding hood, I look like a small

           girl in a hospitalized gorilla

costume. When the horses run out of

      water, we bury them next to a bridge

embankment and walk to the roof of an

Amoco station to watch what you

have been calling our premeditated *Sheva*

Brachot. The first truck that drives

through our take-down never makes it

to the exit. *It looks like a chair on fire towing*

a line of televisions in a marathon, you say. *That's*

too easy, I say. *You're right,* you say. *It looks*

like a rioting nursing home—there are

the overweight orderlies. There is the terrified

food service manager. There, you say,

holding my shin between your damp

thighs, *there is a man without dentures*

believing he isn't.

HYPOTHETICAL INSTRUCTIONS FOR INDIVIDUAL ESCAPE

Take a field of land
workers. Bring them

to a warehouse full of
cold plastic mannequins
and while they are

distracted sell away
their tools. Pocket

the money. Leave
the warehouse, lock
the doors, cut the

power, spend three
days pushing back

the layered foun-
dation, then bury
the lot of it under

a lake. Don't eat for
a week. Imagine pale

faces screaming
beneath the water, but
always keep your

focus. After the fuss
dies down, use the

cash you've gathered
to buy a framed poster
of an aging Kenny

Rogers dressed up
like The Gambler, his

folded arms and pearl-
handled revolver reminding
you of a depressed

dominatrix on her way
to an urban gardening

class. If it gets hard
to live with yourself, talk
to Kenny's beard. Tell

it what you do on the
Internet—that you wish

your neighbors spoke
better English, and that
all of your friends who

are artists come from
parents with advanced

disposable incomes. In
the picture, Kenny's bowtie
will be crooked. His

hair, a terrifying
white. His jeans so well

fitting you'll think of
a thunderous gallop, a
suitcase of dental records

released to a laundromat, a
Peruvian woman shouting, *mi*

médico nunca nos vio nacer!

CAN'T GET NEXT TO JEW

With the conversion Rabbi's voice transmitting through an
earpiece, I walk to the front doors of a rogue abortion

clinic and unravel a sign that stops the protesters from
singing. *Good,* the Rabbi hisses through a field of muffled

static, *that's very good.* Written in pencil, the words we worked
against the poster board seem slightly less effusive than they

had the day before when, after a lunch of uncooked eggs and
lukewarm Manischewitz, we agreed to take more seriously

our failed civilian freedoms. For the rest of that afternoon, we
coughed and gagged and kept our purplish vomit in small

refrigerated Tupperware containers away from the marinating
chicken breasts a member of our congregation had pre-

prepared for Shabbat dinner. *This will make more sense,* the
Rabbi had said, wiping a trail of bruised spittle from the crack

of his dry lips, *when you accept that according to the Torah, it is our
responsibility as the chosen people to illuminate the fallacy of strong*

compelling reason. There were rings around our fingers and we
were rich inside with protein. Later, we stood in separate bath-

rooms drafting slogans for the poster that because of all the
Ambien were never fully finished. I don't remember getting

dressed this morning, but I can see in our sad daylight that
my pleats are creased with syrup and I am staggeringly

bowlegged. Still outside the clinic, I take a breath suggesting
to the Rabbi I am ready. There is a crackle in the speaker, then

the sound of metal cages and the heaviness of steps. *Tape the
sign to your chest*, the Rabbi says. *Okay*, I say. *That's it*, he

says. *Now, walk across the street to where the man is handing out
pamphlets full of bright, discarded fetuses to children by the bank. Okay,*

I say again. *Perfect*, he says. *Without introducing yourself, give him
your sign, take off your shirt, and cut off both your sidelocks with scissors*

from a bris. I do as the Rabbi instructs and everything becomes
quiet. Once we gain a crowd of onlookers, a young woman

holding a dented shoebox and a notarized letter pushes to the
front. *Is this true?* I say, looking closely at his handwriting, *I must*

remove its head? Yes, the Rabbi says. *But why?* I say. *Because*, the
Rabbi says, *it will show your wife that you believe in what we call*

direction. For a while he is laughing as I hold a weak-breasted
robin in the center of my left hand. *You have to trust me*, the

Rabbi finally says. *I guess*, I say, *but I'm not exactly sure this isn't
just a competition. I'm not exactly sure that this is how it ends.*

ABSENT HEALING SONNET

We climb into a hole you've dug in the

    lawn and wait for the results of our

digressive national consumption poll. Because you

    are no longer the mayor, we have

drugs and booze and voter intimidation

    confetti prepared for a well-deserved

celebration, but when we hear the emergency

    cannon fire at the courthouse, it's clear

we didn't find a successful way to lose. Over

    the next seven hours, the towns-

people come to our graveyard

    headquarters with signs and shaved

genitals to show support for your bold

    elemental contrition. One by one we help

them let down. The barber. The banker. The

           teacher, the widow, the geriatric Olympic

water farmer on dialysis. Regardless of how we

        stand impacted, our plot is not big enough

for the dishes or the necessary communal

           ambulance carrier. You try to hand out

shovels, but I hold back your eyes and the

        wrists of a lawyer and together we watch

our sad breath gnaw against the evening like a band of

          evil angels. Everyone else is sleeping when you

finally make your announcement. *Listen*, you say, *we*

     are a small Japanese ocean running

from the cops. I know, I say. *Really*, you say, *we are*

        stiff wet boards and our house is not collapsing.

AN EXERCISE IN MEDIOCRITY

I held your hand while   you stepped into
        the mouth of a   sedated lion. The animal
trainer we had   with us at the time assured
    me the tranquilizers   would render the beast
ineffective until   long after we'd taken our
        souvenir photographs, but   when his tongue
rolled back and I   saw his erect penis, I let
    you deal with your   faith and belief in legitimate
non-believing all   on your own. Since then I've
        sat at this veterinary   clinic huffing cat
dander while   the doctors continue to
    tell me they   still think they can set you
free. To pay for the care I   hope you are receiving, I
        emptied your inheritance and   slept with a female
department store   manager's nametag on in
    hopes of teaching myself   something about
the nature of misappropriated   idealism. Listen, if
        this was intended to be   some kind of masculinity
test, I'm   sorry I kept your tampon
    wrappers in my   safe deposit box but
since your father died   I've been looking for ways
        to keep you naturally   close. I feel sometimes that
I am a costume of trees   in a dramatized
    reenactment of the   1987 San Bernardino
fires. When I sense it   coming, I remember that
        behind my stomach is   a sea of hanging daggers
and I am nothing   nothing   nothing on
                this wire without your weight.

WATCHING OPRAH SHOOT A RIFLE

In late September I had a
dream. We were on a train, buried
in Europe, more money in our
pockets than your father
left you after he died. There
was a man a few rows ahead
of us sleeping in a Roman
candle costume, but halfway
through the dream he stopped
being in focus and suddenly
we were on camels somewhere
in the suburbs. Your birthmarks
were gone and I had gained
substantial weight. Surrounded
by tan strip malls, we wore
ourselves around pylons of
misfired engines—all the metal
gone scorch, the smoke
in bull-pillars, no rising horizon
save shaved birds on a water
tower. I didn't talk much but you
sang to your camel from what I
assume is an extensive pre-surgery
psalm book—*let me down*, you
warbled. *Let me down easy. Let me
down easy my humiliated gate.*

IF LOVING JEW IS WRONG, I DON'T WANT TO BE RIGHT

After I finish re-watching the director's cut of *Love Actually*
on DVD, I send the conversion Rabbi a text message: IM NT

SUR THIS IS WRKG. I make some tea, and by the time it's done
steeping, he's sent the following response: SHUT UP U

BBY. Immediately, I begin drafting a statement of opposition,
supporting my claims with clear, precise evidence, but before

I can finish the line about my sustained growth and maturity,
another message comes through: SHES NT WRTH IT. IS 2, I

respond. UR FOOLNG YRSLF, he answers. AM NOT, I say, O
CMON, he writes quickly, this time sending a picture with his

text, something that looks like the hem of a skirt, or quarters
of king salmon placed in a circle. I try to call the Rabbi, but

it's no use. The messages continue throughout the night and
at just after one thirty-five in the morning, I agree to meet

him at a mannequin warehouse. When I pull into the loading
zone, my headlights scan what I quickly understand to be a

reenactment of a typical Shabbat dinner. The female models
are striking in their resemblance to my mother and sister, but

the one the Rabbi has chosen to represent my father is clearly
a child, its small frame carefully placed on a pile of old tires,

rising just slightly above the spool of copper wire being used
as a table. Once I'm out of the car, the Rabbi asks me to

practice telling my family what we've been discussing. *Okay*, I
say. *Now*, the Rabbi says. *I'm going*, I say. *Spit it out*, he says, and

then I throw a punch. After the Rabbi stops laughing, I let it
all go. *She's good to me*, I say to the female mannequins. *She*

cooks, doesn't have any diseases, and from what I can tell based
on our conversations, she's open to the idea of attending a Seder. Do you

think they'll be this quiet when you really tell them? the Rabbi asks,
playing with a loose wig resting in his lap. I close my eyes. *I*

am a man in a grocery store, buying up bananas, I say. *I'm not sure I*
follow, the Rabbi says. *I am a tall man in a grocery store and I am*

buying all the bananas. It is a wonderful grocery store. I will stay here
forever.

NOTES

The epigraph is from the short story "I Would Have Saved Them if I Could," written by Leonard Michaels.

"The Admittance of Personal Investment" contains information once found on the following websites:

    http://holocaust-history.org/revisionism-isnt/
    http://students.umf.maine.edu/~burtonba/UnitSite/facts
    http://library.thinkquest.org/3300/Dates

"Poem for my Father" is a reimagining of my father's escape from Baghdad in 1970. While it owes a great deal of debt to his experience (both to what he's shared and what he's withheld), the poem is dedicated to all those who have suffered in Iraq, and to anyone who has faced imprisonment, abuse, murder, or forced exodus from their homeland because of their beliefs and traditions—whatever they may be.

"Absent Healing Sonnet" is a translation/interpretation of the poem "Gyroscope," written by Caryl Pagel.

ACKNOWLEDGMENTS

Grateful acknowledgment is made to the following publications in which some of these poems first appeared: *Burdock Magazine, Columbia Poetry Review, Court Green, Fence, iO: A Journal of New American Poetry, Iowa Review, jubilat, Konundrum Engine Literary Review, MAKE Literary Magazine, Malpaís Review,* and *notnostrums.*

This book would not be possible without the support and encouragement of my friends and family:

For your generosity and kindness, thank you to Kate Conlow, Amber Dermont, Nick Dybek, Michelle Falkoff, Kevin González, Zach Isom, Dora Malech, Amy and Selma Margolis, Sevy Perez, Kristen Radtke, Marc Rahe, Alli Rockwell, Zach Savich, and Justin Schoen.

For your keen eyes and editorial insights, thank you to Jason Livingston, Madeline McDonnell, Alyssa Perry, Hilary Plum, Andy Stallings, and Vinnie Wilhelm.

For your patience and vision, thank you to Caryl Pagel.

For your guidance and advice, thank you to James Galvin.

For your attention and care, thank you to Dave Eggers, Jesse Nathan, and the entire staff at McSweeney's.

For your relentless commitment to this project (and for reminding me that "dissonance is an integral part of harmony"), thank you to Dominic Luxford, the hardest working editor I know.

For your collective love and motivation, thank you to Jenny, Phil, Mia, and Zara Blumberg.

And for your belief that this could happen, thank you to my parents, Nashi and Bobbi Khalastchi: אין אהבה גדולה מזו

ABOUT THE AUTHOR

Daniel Khalastchi is a graduate of the Iowa Writers' Workshop. He is the author of *Manoleria* (2011), winner of the Tupelo Press First Book Prize, and his poems have appeared in publications such as *Colorado Review, Denver Quarterly, H_NGM_N, Iowa Review, jubilat, Ninth Letter, Octopus Magazine, 1913: A Journal of Forms,* and *Best American Experimental Writing 2014.* A former fellow at the Fine Arts Work Center in Provincetown, Daniel is currently the associate director of the University of Iowa's Frank N. Magid Center for Undergraduate Writing. He lives in Iowa City and is the co-founder and managing editor of Rescue Press.

THE McSWEENEY'S POETRY SERIES

1. *Love, an Index* by Rebecca Lindenberg (2012).

2. *Fragile Acts* by Allan Peterson (2012).

3. *City of Rivers* by Zubair Ahmed (2012).

4. *x* by Dan Chelotti (2013).

5. *The Boss* by Victoria Chang (2013).

6. *TOMBO* by W. S. Di Piero (2014).

7. *Morning in Serra Mattu: A Nubian Ode* by Arif Gamal (2014).

8. *Saint Friend* by Carl Adamshick (2014).

9. *Tradition* by Daniel Khalastchi (2015).

THE

McSWEENEY'S POETRY SERIES

The McSweeney's Poetry Series is founded on the idea that good poems can come in any style or form, by poets of any age anywhere. Our goal is to publish the best, most vital work we can find, regardless of pedigree. We're after poems that move, provoke, inspire, delight—poems that tear a hole in the sky. And when we find them, we'll publish them the only way we know how: in beautiful hardbacks, with original artwork on the cover. These are books to own, books to cherish, books to loan to friends only in rare circumstances.

⟫⟫⟫——⟪⟪⟪

SUBSCRIPTIONS

The McSweeney's Poetry Series subscription includes our next four books for only $45—around $11 per book—delivered to your door, shipping included. You can sign up at store.mcsweeneys.net.

⟫⟫⟫——⟪⟪⟪

PREVIOUS TITLES

Saint Friend by Carl Adamshick
"Adamshick's way with a glancing aside can hit
you like a truck." —Patton Oswalt

TOMBO by W. S. Di Piero
"A superb poet." —Gerald Stern

Morning in Serra Mattu: A Nubian Ode by Arif Gamal
"Each poem in *Morning in Serra Mattu* is an epistle
of longing and memory." —Yusef Komunyakaa

x by Dan Chelotti
"What is *x*? It is a revelation to read." —Dorothea Lasky